Jean-Philippe Delhomme
Jean-Marc Savoye

THE SUNNY DAYS OF VILLA SAVOYE

Birkhäuser
Basel

THE SUNNY DAYS

The light was pure and limpid. A brisk breeze swept the setting sun's silhouetted ochre clouds. It was a June evening, 2000 or 2001, I'm not sure any longer. I was there, on that patio, next to my mother, and we were listening to chamber music playing Dvořák, Grieg, and Beethoven. A rare and fleeting moment of perfect harmony. One minute, I was at home. One minute, my mother was swept up by her past. After all, everything began here when she and my father were engaged, in this house, in the spring of 1939.

The music stopped. The night had swallowed up the clouds, and the falling dampness brought us back to reality. Time had really gone by.

What had possessed my grandmother to make an appointment, probably for herself alone, on June 8, 1928*, with Le Corbusier? The answer to that question, more complex than it appears, is exactly what this book sets out to provide. I know that my grandmother had seen photos of Le Corbusier houses. She had discovered his work, she recounted, in a magazine she was leafing through on a train ride with a friend: "Look, here's a house I'd love." Long afterwards, when she spoke of "Poissy," which is what she called this villa in the family, she explained that she wanted to build a house that would survive her.

OF VILLA SAVOYE

* Like much of the information in this book, this date was taken from the remarkable book – a really colossal amount of work – called "Les Heures claires" that Josep Quetglas devoted to the Villa Savoye. Unfortunately, this book exists only in a Spanish version (cf. Bibliography).

I mention my grandmother because she was the driving force behind this project, choosing modernity over a manor or an imposing and opulent chateau, the types of home that her history, her culture, and her milieu would have more naturally led her to buy. But in 1928 what she wanted was to build and look resolutely toward the future. She even planned, in her first letter to Le Corbusier, for it to be "possible to enlarge the house in a few years without ruining it." This was, in fact, the letter sent in the summer of 1928 that commissioned the work. Written by hand without any flourishes, its style was very surprising. It almost looked like a draft, as there was no formal greeting, which in itself was quite unusual. The last page may have been lost, but the fact that this letter was found in the Le Corbusier archives is proof that it was sent. The orders were detailed and precise. At first reading, it didn't look as if much latitude would be given to the architect. Considering my grandmother's recollections, I didn't find this surprising: she knew very well what she wanted, and she was not easily taken in.

Even more than the form, it is the content of this letter that deserves attention, because in construction matters, and particularly for individual houses, the client is very important. It is the client who determines what they want, since it is the client who is going to live there, eat, sleep, love, laugh, cry, and share everything there with the family. This very practical dimension must not be neglected when considering my grandparents' demands. They were not putting forward a manifesto or being philanthropic; they were simply building a country house in which to be happy. If my grandmother had heard of a "machine for living", the June appointment would have ended there.

«I WOULD LIKE TO BE ABLE TO EXTEND IT IN A FEW YEARS WITHOUT THAT EXTENSION DAMAGING THE HOUSE» E. SAVOYE

Monsieur

Voici les principaux détails de ce que je désire avoir dans la maison de campagne
D'abord, je voudrais qu'il soit possible de l'agrandir dans quelques années sans que l'agrandissement abîme la maison
Il y a une l'eau chaude et froide, le gaz, l'électricité (lumière et force) le chauffage central.
Au rez-de-chaussée 1 grande pièce de 12 m/7, 1 vestiaire (lavabo-water), 1 cuisine 1 office. 1 fruitier 1 chambre à coucher 8/4, une autre chambre à coucher 4/4 séparées par une salle de bain avec water
A l'étage ma chambre 5/ avec grande salle de bain water fermé, 1 lingerie et 1 boudoir de 15 m².
Service : 2 chambres de bonnes avec prise d'eau et un water. 1 garage pour 3 voitures. 1 logement de concierge et un logement de chauffeur. 1 débarras pour outils et un grenier (malles)
1 cave à vin et une autre cave.

Détails : Une cuisine comme à Ville d'Avray avec 3 prises de courant force et 2 éclairages
Un office un peu plus grand que celui de Ville d'Avray à un emplacement pour la lessiveuse électrique et une prise de courant force.
Un vestiaire assez grand avec une lampe au plafond et une autre au lavabo.
Dans la grande pièce, éclairage indirect et flambeaux sur la table pour manger. 5 prises de courant une grande cheminée. Il ne faut pas que cette salle soit strictement rectangulaire, mais comporte des coins confortables

---

Dear Sir,
Here are the main details of what I'm looking for in a country house. Firstly, I would like to be able to extend it in a few years without that extension damaging the house.

It needs to have hot and cold running water, a gas supply, electricity (for both light and power) and central heating. <u>On the ground floor</u> there should be 1 large room measuring 12×7m, 1 cloakroom (with a sink and running water), 1 kitchen, 1 pantry, 1 fruit store, 1 bedroom measuring 8×4m and another separate bedroom measuring 4×4m separated by a bathroom ~~with a toilet~~.

<u>On the first floor</u> should be my bedroom measuring 5×4m with a large bathroom, a separate toilet and 1 boudoir measuring 15m².

<u>Service areas:</u> 2 bedrooms for maids with running water and a toilet. 1 garage with space for 3 cars. Accommodation for 1 site manager and 1 driver. 1 storage room for tools and an attic.

1 wine cellar and another separate cellar.

Details: A kitchen like that at the Ville d'Avray with 3 power sockets and 2 lamps. A pantry slightly larger than the one at the Ville d'Avray with space for the electric washing machine and a power socket.

A fairly large cloakroom with one overhead lamp and another by the sink.

In the large room there should be discreet lighting and candlesticks on the dining table. 5 power sockets, a large fireplace, this room does not necessarily need to be rectangular but should have comfortable areas.

1 chambre au coucher 5/ pour mon fils faisant chambre et bureau avec éclairage au lit, au bureau et au milieu - prise de courant.
Salle de bain avec une grande glace contre le mur et un éclairage au dessus et l'au lavabo — ~~Water séparé~~
armoire à linge et à costumes.
1 chambre à coucher 2 lits pour les amis - éclairage au lit. et au milieu. prise de courant. Toilette
A l'étage chambre à 2 lits 5/ - éclairage indirect lampe électrique à chaque lit et 1/2 prise de courant grande salle de bain éclairage et prise de courant au lavabo, grande glace contre le mur éclairage à la glace.
1 boudoir à côté de la chambre
1 lingerie 1.50/ armoires de chaque côté à glissière
table rabattante 3 de 1m20 et la fenêtre, lumière au dessus de la table et prise de courant force pour repasser
Lumière au plafond.
Logement jardinier 2 pièces cuisine water
garage 3 voitures avec eau et lumière et logement du chauffeur au dessus 2 pièces cuisine et water grenier.

A voir - tapis de caoutchouc ou parquet dans les chambres - carrelages partout ailleurs.
Armoires à provision - Serrures Yale
Isolant pour les murs extérieurs - contre les chaleurs et le froid
Devis descriptif - quantitatif - estimatif
Tous les travaux en supplément ou en diminution seront établis sur le prix de série de base du forfait.

A 5×4m bedroom for my son which he can also use as an office with a power socket in the center.
Bathroom with a large mirror on the wall with overhead lighting above and a sink also with a light. ~~Separate toilet~~ Wardrobes for linen and suits.
1 bedroom with 2 single beds for guests. Lighting over the bed and in the middle of the room. Power socket, toilet.
Upstairs: 5×4m bedroom with 2 single beds, indirect lighting, electric lamps for each bed and 2 power sockets, large bathroom with lighting and a power socket next to the sink, large mirror on the wall with lighting.
1 boudoir next to the bedroom
1 2.5×3m linen cupboard on each side with sliding doors
1.2m-high fold-out table by the window, a lamp above the table and a power socket for ironing
Ceiling light.
Accommodation for the gardener, 2 rooms plus a kitchen and toilet.

A 3-car garage with a water tap and light and with accommodation for a driver upstairs, 2 rooms plus a kitchen and toilet.
To check: are there rubber-backed carpets or parquet in the bedrooms? Tiles should be used everywhere else. Food store—Yale locks. Insulated exterior walls—to protect against the heat and cold.
Descriptive, quantitative, itemized quote. All the work adding or removing elements should be established according to normal industry rates.

The apartment building in which the Savoye family lived, at No. 105, rue de Courcelles

The first striking thing is that she did not want an enormous house. It was designed for three people: my grandparents and their only son. It had to have two bedrooms and one other, only one other, for friends. It is one hour, or an hour and a half, from Paris and they would come by car or by train for the day. This was a far cry from a great mansion designed for vacations overflowing with people. The family was small. My grandfather had distant relations with his brothers and sisters, and my grandmother barely saw her sister, who remained in northern France. Of course, there was my father, who would undoubtedly get married one day, but for the moment he was twenty-one, and if he had children, there would be time to enlarge the house without "ruining" it. In any case, I can vouch for the fact that my grandmother was not one to let herself be overwhelmed by a horde of grandchildren to whom she would be singing nursery rhymes before putting them to bed. No, family was not my grandparents' major preoccupation, and that came through in this first letter. It would also come through in the plans. Of course, staff was envisaged: three bedrooms on the ground floor, probably one for a chambermaid and one for a cook. And a third for the chauffeur, who had his own entrance. The gardener would live in an outbuilding.

As far as the house was concerned, it had to be comfortable and bright. Lighting, outlets, and electric power sockets for the installation of new machines – and, above all, for an electric wash boiler – are mentioned more than twenty times in this two-page letter. Heating is, of course, "central", but my grandmother nevertheless wanted a fireplace in the main living room, which should not be "rigidly rectangular but have comfortable areas." She even thought about using rubber carpet for the bedroom floors. The kitchen should be "as big as the one in Ville d'Avray" and the pantry even bigger. This was an important sentence. I wasn't surprised by my grandmother's interest in the kitchen, because she loved to cook, but the sentence also shows that she had visited the "Villa Church" that Le Corbusier had just finished in Ville d'Avray.

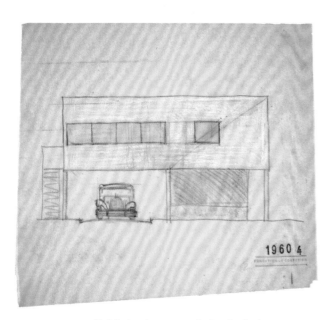

Sketch showing a car parked under the house

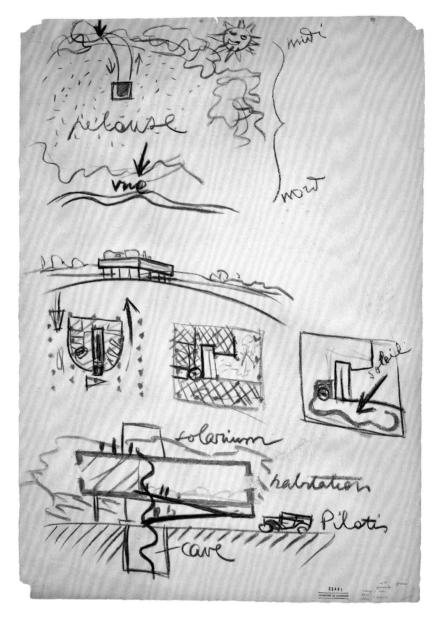

Drawings by Le Corbusier for a conference in
Buenos Aires (1929), reprinted in *Précisions*

Calling on Le Corbusier meant that my grandmother knew what to expect and had clearly opted for a modern house. That is what comes through in this letter. An astonishing modernity wells up in this almost ordinary document, without it being obvious: the family is already nuclear; you go by car, you travel back and forth to Paris in the same day; and while women have help, they cook if they want to. They also practice sports. An excellent swimmer – she swam across the bay of Saint-Jean-de-Luz – my grandmother, like my grandfather, adored playing golf.

My grandparents were neither very cultured, nor far-seeing, nor fascinated by progress, but they were modern, deeply modern. This was not posturing, nor a statement of principle; it was simply the way they lived. These were the grounds on which Le Corbusier and they would get together. They left him great latitude, and the architect said of them that they "were without any preconceived ideas." This is clearly of importance, and these unusual clients deserve to be described in more detail.

While Pierre and Eugénie Savoye were free, rich, and serene in 1928, it had not always been thus. First there was the Great War. My grandfather, whom I never knew, was thirty-four in 1914 and had one son, my father, who was seven. He was drafted and served for the four years of the war. His age and the fact that he was a father protected him from serving on the front, but the war was nevertheless horrific. Like all the men who got out alive, he was marked for life. He retained from this war the idea that the Germans, who had already invaded and conquered France in 1870, would always return, and it served no purpose to be owner of a house that would inevitably be destroyed. And with a guarded smile he always added that insurance companies never reimbursed war damages. He knew what he was talking about. He did not know to what degree history would prove him right.

Roger, the son of Pierre and Eugénie Savoye

Dear Sir,

Enclosed you will find the (blue) prints from the 3rd survey of your house in Poissy.

We have included the reductions needed to fit with the suggested price.
Mr. Cormier has the new plans.

We request that you sign the two enclosed copies of our contract, one of which you should keep for your records.

An increase in our workload led us to overlook this correspondence which we spoke about at the beginning of our dealings.

We can start the work as soon as we receive your initial payment. Yours faithfully,

Letter to the Savoye family sent with the third plan, signed Jeanneret on December 21, 1928

Faithful to this principle, he was a lifelong renter; the Villa Savoye was the only house he ever owned. Or, to be precise, he did buy two farms that he gave to his wife. They were as much gifts as investments, because my grandmother believed in the land and liked trees and growing things. Born in Lille in January 1888 – she was three months younger than Le Corbusier – she was an intelligent, vibrant, and authoritarian woman. Clearly, she had a difficult childhood, as her parents divorced and her mother remarried. Being the child of divorced parents in the French provinces in the late nineteenth century was not simple. Later on, her father's family, and above all her uncles, who were very rich and childless, rejected my grandfather for obscure reasons, thereby depriving her of a rich inheritance. She nevertheless did what she wanted and succeeded in marrying the man she would deeply love.

On my grandfather's side, he was from the bourgeoisie of the north of France. The oldest of six siblings, he found himself at eighteen years of age, following the death of his father in 1898, at the head of the family business, a once-prosperous brewery and buyer and seller of hops. The business rapidly declined and the family experienced serious financial setbacks that altered family relations.

In 1906, when my grandfather got married, he was still a hops merchant. The next year, for reasons unknown, he moved into insurance in partnership with a family from Lille, bringing insurance brokerage to France from Great Britain, where it was a well-developed activity. Around 1918, this business began to prosper and grow very quickly.

By 1928, he was rich, but he was no Croesus, and his wealth was recent. His work monopolized his time completely, and he thus devoted little attention to the house construction. This was clearly his wife's project, even if he was attentive to the choice of companies and the costs of construction. He decided on the general contractor Cormier.

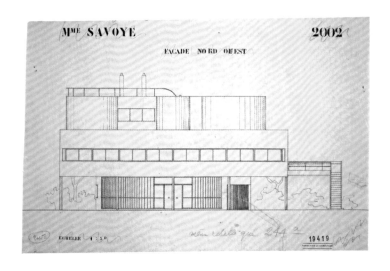

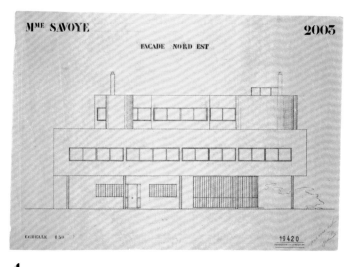

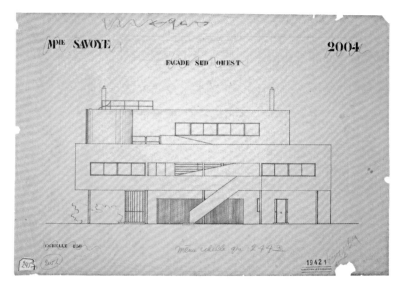

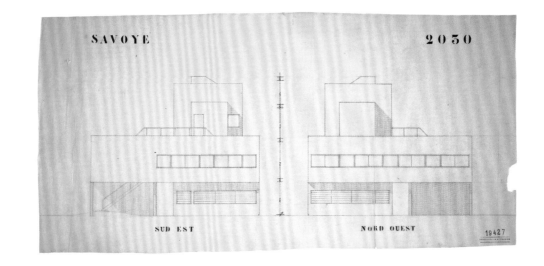

SAVOYE

2030

SUD EST

NORD OUEST

19427

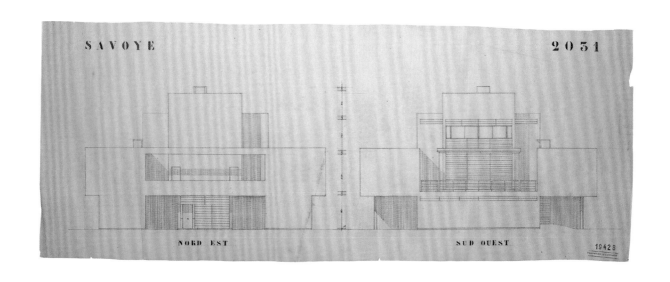

SAVOYE

2031

NORD EST

SUD OUEST

19428

An artistic impression produced by the
Le Corbusier workshop

245

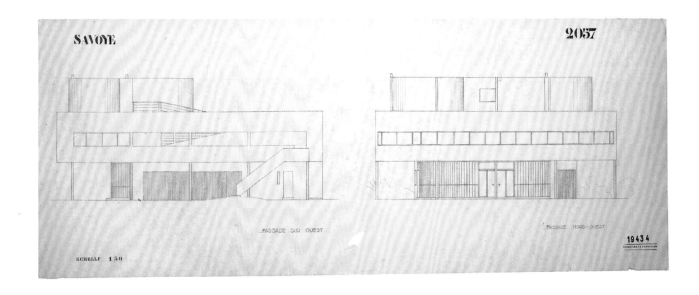

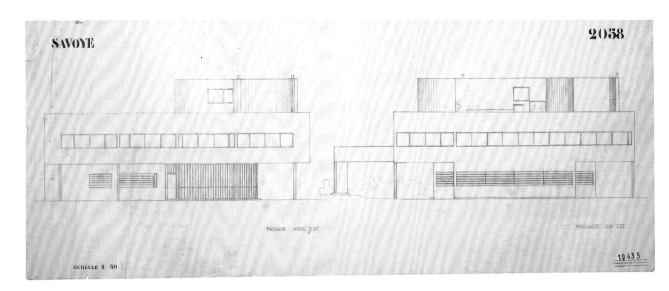

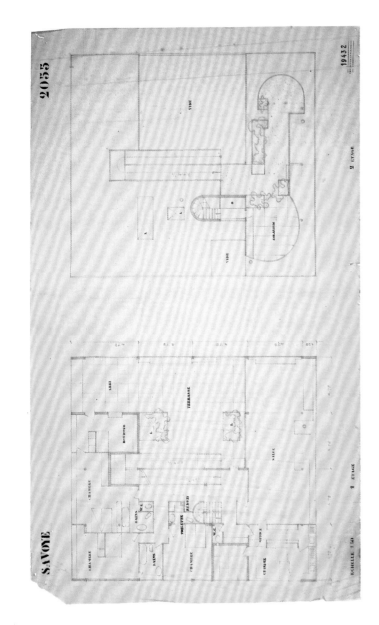

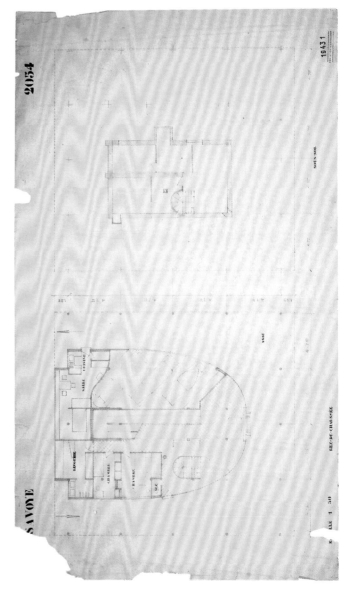

As for my grandmother, who had undergone an operation in 1924 serious enough to warrant drawing up a detailed will, she was now in great shape. The old family issues were behind her. Their only son was growing up. He was twenty-one and seemed ready to take over from his father one day. In short, in this month of June 1928, everything was going well in my grandparents' life. My grandmother was forty years old and beautiful. Her husband was forty-eight and wildly successful. They had the future in their hands. France had been at peace for the last ten years, and it was thriving in the effervescence of the Roaring Twenties. The coast was clear. It was the time of Sunny Days, the name* they gave to this house.

Surely that is one of the keys to the beauty of the house. The clients the architect had before him wanted a country house that corresponded to this blessed moment of their existence. They wanted time stopped. They wanted light, and wanted to enjoy all of this to the utmost. Everything had to be simple, practical, modern, and comfortable, and that would be seen in the plans.

A first plan was presented to my grandparents in October 1928. It was refused because, among other issues, it was too expensive. A month later a second plan was prepared, and that too was rejected. The third plan, close to the first, was accepted but without its third floor. It changed a great deal during the work, but its acceptance launched the construction. It was assessed at 558,690 French francs, considerably lower than the first estimate at 851,520 francs. There would be many extensions, and in the end the house probably cost what had been specified in the first plans.

* In French, Les Heures claires

As we have already seen in the order letter, my grandmother had very specific demands that were indicative of her desire for the comfort mentioned earlier, including electricity and central heating, of course. But I keep wondering about the bathroom. My grandmother wanted a big mirror that she did not get. But what did she think of that mosaic bathtub that you had to climb down into and that seemed to be imitating a Turkish bath? And what about that lounge area in the shape of a chaise longue that Le Corbusier had designed a few months earlier with Charlotte Perriand? Did my grandmother lounge around there after a steaming bath, or did she languorously wait there for her husband to take his?

And how about the lack of a partition between the bedroom and the bathroom, separated merely by a sliding curtain, as if there were no frontier between space for getting dressed, for resting, and for pleasure? An obvious, almost joyous, sensuality exudes from this area that contrasts with the clean lines of this quite austere house. Without transgressing good taste, I like to imagine that my grandparents knew how to enjoy life.

The bathroom seen from the bedroom

Another surprising aspect was the importance of the car. We know that Le Corbusier loved cars and understood the deep transformation they would bring about in people's lives. He expressed this notion in 1930 in an article for a German magazine: "The house is thus to be determined at the very least by a new factor, the automobile." Here, too, the architect's vision resonated perfectly with my grandparents' desires. Of course, it was Le Corbusier who thought of pilotis, but the idea of arriving by car and parking in the house without having to back in or accomplish other maneuvers was surely encouraged by my grandmother. She was very proud of her driver's license, which she got in 1924, but she was a lousy driver, and I have only to think of her in the 1960s driving her Peugeot 203 to understand how appreciative she must have been not to have to go into reverse!

A note on the garage and the chauffeur's bedroom: The garage had to house three cars – my grandmother's, my grandfather's, and the one my father would surely have. That was a lot for a three-person family in 1928. But my grandmother was independent and intended to be able to go to Poissy whenever she wanted. As for my grandfather, who had witnessed his brother Jean's death from the recoil of the crank, with himself at the wheel – these were the dark hours – he no longer drove. He had a chauffeur, who thus had to have a bedroom.

Construction lasted all through 1929. My grandparents followed the work attentively and we have the record of what they said on the width of the doors they thought too narrow or the thickness of the walls they considered too thin. There does not seem to have been any major incident. Le Corbusier regularly asked to be paid, but there was nothing exceptional in that. When my grandmother criticized how the driveway to the house was built, Le Corbusier said she was right and wrote to the general contractor to order him to satisfy his clients, saying: "Mr. Savoye is the nicest client we have ever had" (letter of July 17, 1930).

Were my grandparents aware of the exceptional house they were constructing? Maybe not, but they never attempted to change the plans, and they were not put out by what was emerging from the earth. My grandmother even found the lighting for the main room in the house in a factory showroom.

As for Le Corbusier himself, he had an inkling that he was building a remarkable work. He wrote to his mother on February 21, 1929: "We're digging the hole for a beautiful villa in Poissy." On April 25, 1930, we again feel his enthusiasm. This time he wrote to his mother: "The house in Poissy is becoming a little miracle. It is a creation."

In a letter of December 31, 1929, the general contractor Cormier deemed the work finished. But there were undoubtedly still many things to take care of. The rubber carpet for the ramp had not been installed as of September 1930, but this did not stop my grandparents from moving in. They received a card from Le Corbusier, dated June 28, 1930, in which he writes, "I was happy to see your house so well lived in."

« THE HOUSE IN POISSY IS BECOMING A LITTLE MIRACLE.
IT IS A CREATION » LE CORBUSIER

Were they happy there? It is a difficult question to answer. There are no documents, no photos, and no films that attest to it. What is certain is that they enjoyed playing golf. My mother remembered my grandfather replaying the great putt he had made on the lawn in front of the house. They were members of the nearby Saint-Germain golf course club for years.

They were also happy to see their friends from the north of France with whom they had business relations, and it is these relations that explain how they came to be in Poissy in the first place. My grandfather insured the Kuhlmann company, undoubtedly the biggest French chemical business of the time, established in Lille since the early nineteenth century. The Kuhlmann family had built a considerable empire, spanning chemistry to banking; they had founded the bank Crédit du Nord. In 1928 the Kuhlmann establishment bought up the estate of Villiers, a beautiful nineteenth-century chateau surrounded by a 135-acre park. It was the head of Kuhlmann who told my grandfather: "Pierre, as you're looking for a plot to build a house, come to Poissy and I will turn over a part of the estate we have just bought."

That is how the Villiers estate came to be divided into three plots. Seventy acres remained with the château, which became a place for the employees of the Kuhlmann empire; seventy acres were bought by the Agache family, a very big spinning family from the north, linked by marriage to the Kuhlmanns; and seventeen acres went to my grandparents. The Agache construction was immense. It was in fact several houses, in a neo-Norman half-timbered style with corner towers – beautiful workmanship, as luxurious and classic as it was boring. Thus, on the heights of Poissy overlooking a stunning view of the Seine was created a locus where the bourgeoisie of the north spent their weekends. They entertained each other, had friends to visit, and, of course, cultivated useful relations for doing business.

In this little world, my grandfather was the one who had the most to gain, as it could be said, if an anachronism can be excused, that he was at the head of a thriving startup that could only prosper in the shadow of this dynasty comprising richer and more powerful people than himself.

In the spring of 1939, my parents' engagement was one of the last happy moments in the house. Celebrated in the privacy of the two families, it prompted this judgment from my mother's father, a Bordeaux lawyer, a judgment as definitive and peremptory as he was himself: "My dear, I pity you becoming part of a family who could have such a house built."

But what also marked these years and probably spoiled some of the pleasure of living in the house were the defects my grandmother never stopped complaining about. Letters of complaint followed one another in relentless succession. The heating was a major problem. My grandparents were worried in 1934 and sent for an engineer friend, who looked at the situation and made suggestions that were implemented. The stakes were high, because my father spent a year in a sanatorium and could not withstand the cold during the winter. Then there was the troublesome problem of damp. My grandmother wrote to Le Corbusier on September 7, 1936, saying: "It's raining on the ramp, it's raining in the garage and the garage wall is completely soaked."

Her irritation is palpable, and it rose as time passed. Exactly one year later, September 7, 1937, she wrote again, fed up that her complaining appeared to be futile: "You're always sending me visitors and not answering my letters." By October 11 of the same year, she was really getting angry. After telling the architect that his decennial liability was at stake – you can sense the insurance expert's wife who knows what she's talking about – she added: "It is urgent that you make [this house] habitable. I would hope it will not be necessary to have recourse to legal means."

September 7th, 1936

Sir,

I hope you are now back after your holidays and that you will be able to come to Poissy.

It's raining in the entrance hall, it's raining on the staircase and the garage wall is completely soaked.

In addition it's still raining in my bathroom, which floods each time it rains. The water is getting in through the roof light.

The gardener also has damp in his walls. I would like to be able to sort all this out while I am still here. I am in Poissy every day this week except on Wednesday afternoon and Thursday morning.

I would prefer that you call to let me know when you plan to come round.

With best wishes.

October 31st, 1937
Mr. Savoye

Dear Sir,

This message follows on from yesterday's letter, dictated on my return from Brussels during a brief period of calm.

I would like to add that:

In the event that the planned developments mean there is still an issue with the north wall, we should fix a wood veneer 3 or 4 cm from the inner face of the wall.

Otherwise, I wish to assure you that we are trying to do our best to satisfy your needs and that you should consider us as friends of your house. Equally, I would like to remain a friend of yours, maintaining a relationship of trust between us. I am and must always remain on good terms with my clients.

31 octobre 1937   177

Monsieur Savoye   M 7 - 12

Cher Monsieur

Ce mot complète ma lettre
d'hier dictée à mon retour de Bruxelles
dans un bref instant disponible.

Il faut ajouter ceci :
Au cas où les aménagements proposés
laisseraient encore persister un manque
de confort au mur nord, nous y
ferions installer un placage de bois
à 3 à 4 cm du mur, à l'intérieur.

Je désire par ailleurs, vous donner
la certitude que nous désirions faire
au mieux pour vous satisfaire et
que vos devez nous considérer comme
les amis de votre maison ; je désirerai
d'autre part demeurer un ami
tout court de vous, nos relations

ayant toujours été de pleine
confiance. Je suis et je
suis toujours demeurer l'ami de
mes clients.

v. dévoué

Le Corbusier

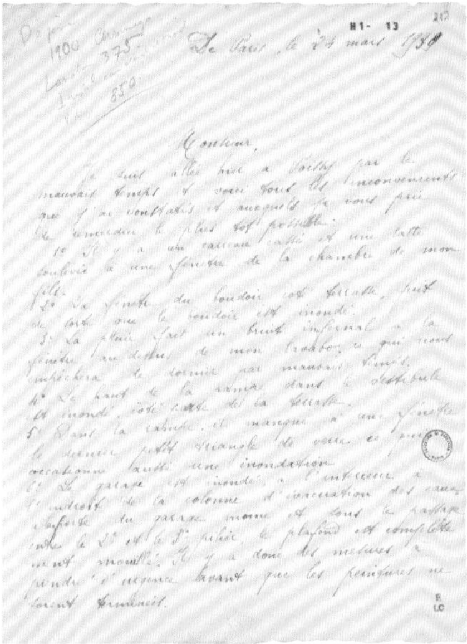

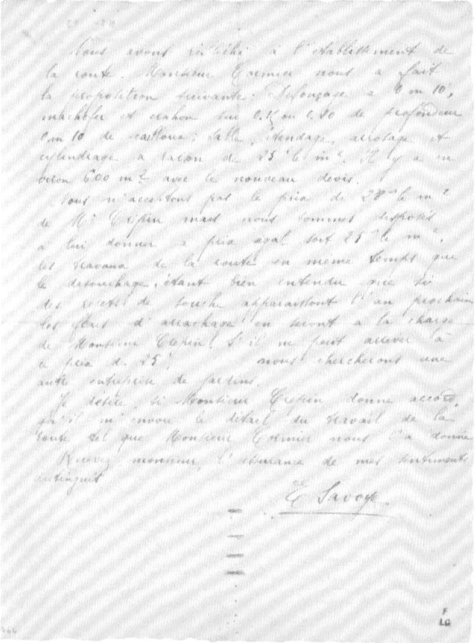

Dear Sir,

I went to Poissy yesterday in bad weather and below are all the problems I identified and which I request you remedy as soon as possible:

1. There is a broken roof tile and a loose wooden board by the window in my son's bedroom.

2. The boudoir window overlooking the terrace leaks so much that the boudoir is flooded.

3. The rain makes a terrible noise at the window above my sink, which is likely to prevent us from sleeping in bad weather.

4. The top of the staircase in the vestibule is flooded, on the side leading to the terrace door.

5. On the staircase, the top small glass triangle is missing from a window, which also causes flooding.

6. The garage is flooded inside where the downpipe runs, by the garage door itself and the whole floor area between the second and third pillars, the ceiling is completely sodden.

Therefore, urgent remedial work is required before the painting is finished.

We have given some thought to building the road. Mr. Cormier has made the following suggestion: dig out the surface to a depth of 0.10m, spread clinker and gypsum to a depth of 0.15 or 0.20m, then small stones to a depth of 0.10m, spread with sand, water and roll for a cost of 25 francs per square meter; there are around 600m² according to the new quotes.

We cannot accept the price of 28 francs per square meter suggested by Mr. Crépin, but we are willing to pay him 25 francs per square meter for the roadworks if he will do it at the same time as he removes the tree roots provided of course that, if further roots appear next year, the cost of removing them will be borne by Mr. Crépin. If he is unable to accept this price of 25 francs, then we will find another landscaping firm.

I ask that, if Mr. Crépin agrees to the price, he send me the details of the roadworks as Mr. Cormier has done.

Yours faithfully

E. Savoye

This blunt letter prompted an uncommon reply on October 31, from Le Corbusier to my grandfather: "You should think of us as friends of your house. And I would very much like to remain a friend of yours."

However, the situation did not improve, and in my grandmother's last known letter to the architect, dated November 4, 1939, she asked him for the house plans so that she did not have to contact his offices every time there were repairs to be made, which was frequently. On top of the recurring problems of heating and damp, my mother said that the Villa was poorly soundproofed and everything could be heard from one room to the next.

In September 1939, shortly after the declaration of war, believing, like so many Parisians, that the German army was about to bomb the capital, the family – my grandparents and my parents, who were expecting their first child – settled in Poissy. My grandfather and my father commuted to work in Paris every day, and my mother killed time as best she could, later recounting how she made friends with the gardener, who fed her enormous pieces of buttered toast that she ate with the garden radishes.

The days were getting shorter, the damp increasing, the cold settling into the unheatable house, and to top it all off, civil defense ordered that all the windows of the house be covered in methylene blue. The ambience was morose. The Villa Savoye's sunny days were over.

Seeing that Paris was not being bombed and that the war, at least for the moment, was not really on, my parents decided to return to Paris around the end of October, followed shortly thereafter by my grandparents.

In May 1940, when the Battle of France began, one might have thought they would again take refuge in Poissy. But it was too close to Paris. For safety's sake, my mother returned to Bordeaux to give birth. My father and grandfather were busy moving their offices into the free zone.

The Germans requisitioned the house, which was ideally situated to oversee the valley of the Seine and the Ford factories a little farther below. Le Corbusier had clearly understood the land (Oeuvre complète 1910–1929, pp. 186–87): "Situated at the top of the dome, [the house] will open its windows to the four horizons. The living quarters floor with its hanging garden rises above the pilotis to take advantage of the panorama spanning the horizon." The Germans couldn't have dreamed of a better observation post, which is why they took over the house. My grandfather was right: the Germans did come back.

After the Germans, it was the Americans who took over the place until late August 1944. They probably used the Villa to store matériel or vehicles, but they do not appear to have lived in it, because it was in very bad shape. In July 1942, my grandfather ordered a certified report: all the radiators had frozen, many of the windowpanes and tiles were broken, all the doors had been broken down, everything that was meant to slide didn't, the floor was ruined as well as the fireplace in the living room, and the house had to be completely repainted. The report attested to many signs of humidity, indicating that the problem of damp had never been solved.

« YOU SHOULD THINK OF US AS FRIENDS OF YOUR HOUSE »
LE CORBUSIER

C E R T I F I C A T E
_____

I, President of the Local Liberation Committee, certify that the property called "Les Heures Claires" belonging to Mr. SAVOYE and located at Chemin de Villiers in Poissy was occupied by German troops during the following periods:
1. from 08.12.1940 to 11.16.1940
2. from 06.01.1941 to 09.17.1941
3. from 11.23.1941 to 03.18.1942
During periods of non-occupation the property remained requisitioned.

The requisition was canceled on 11.09.1942 and the property was then requisitioned once again from 05.15.1944 to 08.25.1944.

The President of the Local
Liberation Committee

Three years later, when my grandparents wanted to get their house back, they found it even more run-down. It was still standing, but it would have had to be redone from top to bottom to be habitable once again. They did not do it, and I have the feeling they never really intended to. It was not a question of money – they had enough. Instead, it was because they knew from experience that the house had been badly built and they would never solve the problems of heating and damp.

And then life went on. In 1945 my grandfather was sixty-five and my grandmother fifty-seven. They did not have as much energy. My parents had three children, and clearly this house was not going to become a family home. Lastly, and this is perhaps the main point in this postwar period, my grandfather did not want to be a homeowner again because the Germans always returned and insurers never reimbursed war damages. And in truth, in spite of official reports and attestations, he was never reimbursed for anything. Still, they did not want to abandon Poissy. Not at all.

In 1947, they made the decision to transform the property into a farm. Right from the beginning, my grandmother had laid out a very big kitchen garden and an orchard abounding in fruit trees. The produce was consumed by the family – jams and jellies were made in the house – and by the gardener and the staff; the surplus was undoubtedly sold to the many market farmers in the vicinity.

The flower and plant garden would become a real farm. We have the very detailed inventory of what was planted at that time: more than two thousand pear trees and almost as many apple. A foreman was hired who would live in the lodge and see to making the farm thrive. The house would serve as a storage place for farm machinery and for the harvest.

«IT IS URGENT THAT YOU MAKE [THIS HOUSE] HABITABLE» E. SAVOYE

That is how this house, so quintessentially modern in its spirit, form, materials, and use, was, in an astonishing paradox, rescued from abandon by the most traditional of activities. My grandfather died in 1950, but that did not have any effect on the future of the Villa; my grandmother continued to come regularly and to play golf at the Saint-Germain club, where she was a member until at least 1959. My brothers and sisters, considerably older than me, remember some of the Sunday picnics on the front lawn when the weather was good.

All of this might have continued for a long time, but the city of Poissy was growing fast. Very near the Villa stretched the new, monotonously white five-story Beauregard housing projects. The nearby and fast-growing car factories had to house their automobile workers, and France to house its baby boom. Then a high school needed to be built.

Around the Beauregard complex there were few constructible plots. In 1957 the minister of education requested the city to find a place. In April of the same year, the mayor of Poissy wrote to my father asking if he would agree to turn over his property to the city. This did eventually occur, but not right away, because in addition to the usual delays, my grandmother did not want to give up Poissy. In an October 7 letter, my father wrote to the mayor: "My mother is not in favor of giving up this property and you will certainly understand that, like me, she is very attached to it, with deep emotional ties, and her cherished desire is to continue to profit from it peacefully during her life." My father, though, did not completely close the door and recognized the general interest of the project. He said he thought that if there were no other available plots, he would be able to convince his mother.

The city followed through in its choice and the expropriation procedure was set in motion, leading to an expropriation order for public utility, dated April 28, 1959. I won't go into the procedure. My father and grandmother would contest the indemnity they were granted. They appealed and were partially successful. It is to be noted that the indemnity for the trees and the farm was higher than that for the house!

At the beginning, the notion of razing the house once and for all in order to construct the high school and its sports facilities was envisaged. But rather quickly, Le Corbusier and a group of architects, some of whom he had worked with, would join forces in a remarkably efficient effort. A temporary committee to save Villa Savoye was created. It launched an international, and very successful, petition, and the lycée was built elsewhere.

The mayor wrote to his lawyer on July 29, 1959: "I would like to notify you that the National Education minister rejected the expropriation and the Minister of Arts and Letters confirmed it. […] Indeed, the Le Corbusier house must remain and in its original setting. The National Education minister has asked me to find another plot for the construction of lycée buildings." However, there was no other plot, and the reality of the new school year had to be confronted – not to mention the Poissy population, which was becoming impatient.

Other than the traditional anonymous, insulting letters to the mayor's office ("Before talking 'art,' talk the DOUGH Le Corbusier earns in his disgusting works"), there were some people who thought priority should be given to children. That is what one could read very clearly in the monthly paper of the Christian community of Beauregard in May 1959: "Le Corbusier's disciples will surely come up with the millions to guarantee a few walls of cement: will the necessary credits be found to help train boys and girls who will be the adults of the year 2000?"

Beauregard Catholic community newsletter,
dated May 1959

An anonymous letter

COMITE PROVISOIRE DE SAUVEGARDE   Paris, le 11 mars 1959.
DE LA VILLA SAVOYE.

La Villa Savoye de LE CORBUSIER à Poissy est en danger.

La Commune a engagé une procédure d'expropriation du
terrain et de la Villa afin de construire un lycée.

La première décision d'expropriation sera prise le
17 de ce mois.

Nous sommes décidés à tout mettre en oeuvre pour empêcher
cet acte de vandalisme.

Nous vous appelons à faire parvenir vos protestations
à l'attaché culturel de votre pays à Paris
et à notre comité de sauvegarde.

Nous vous appelons à soutenir notre action pour assurer
la remise en état de la Villa et pour nous permettre de rechercher
sous la direction de monsieur LE CORBUSIER, une solution définitive
d'affectation pour cette maison.

LE COMITE PROVISOIRE DE SAUVEGARDE
DE LA VILLA SAVOYE

MR. R.AUJAME, W.BODIANSKY, D.CHENUT, N.EFFRONT, J.FLOM,
A.JAEGGLI, A.KOPP, G.LAGNEAU, C.PERRIAND, J.C.PETITDEMANGE,
PREVERAL, H.QUILLÉ, P.RIBOULET, RENAUDIE, E.SCHREIBER-
AUJAME, G.THURNAUER, VERET.

PROVISIONAL PROTECTION COMMITTEE   Paris, March 11th, 1959
    FOR THE VILLA SAVOYE

The LE CORBUSIER — designed Villa Savoye is in danger.

The local authority has initiated an expropriation procedure for
the land and the Villa to build a high school on the site.
The initial decision regarding expropriation will be made on the
17th of this month.

We are determined to do everything possible to prevent this act
of vandalism. We ask that you send your letters of protest to the
cultural attaché representing your country in Paris and a copy to
our protection committee.

We ask that you support our efforts to guarantee the restoration
of the Villa and allow us, with the assistance of Mr. LE
CORBUSIER, to identify a lasting solution for the use of this
house.

PROVISIONAL PROTECTION
COMMITTEE FOR THE VILLA SAVOYE

MR. R. AUJAME, W. BODIANSKY, D. CHENUT, N. EFFRONT, J. FLOM,
A. JAEGGLI, A. KOPP, G. LAGNEAU, C. PERRIAND, J.C. PETITDEMANGE,
PREVERAL, H. QUILLÉ, P. RIBOULET, RENAUDIE, E. SCHREIBER-
AUJAME, G. THURNAUER, VERET.

An international petition by seventeen architects to
safeguard the Villa Savoye, begun in March 1959

LE MINISTRE D'ÉTAT

CHARGÉ DES AFFAIRES CULTURELLES

PARIS, LE 20 Mai 1960

3, RUE DE VALOIS

Monsieur LE CORBUSIER
Architecte
35, rue de Sèvres
PARIS

23 Mai 1960

Cher Le Corbusier,

     Bernard Anthonioz suit
très attentivement les opérations admi-
nistratives qui concernent la villa
Savoye , et pourra faire le point avec
vous .

     Bien amicalement .

André MALRAUX

F
LC

A letter from André Malraux to Le Corbusier from
May 20, 1960

Le Corbusier followed all this attentively. In a letter of March 10, 1959, my father brought him up to date on the expropriation procedure and gave him the figures at stake. My father clearly accepted the inevitability of expropriation, but he preferred to be compensated by the Ministry of Culture and that the house not be destroyed. I know that through one of his best friends he approached Saint-Gobain, which might have created a foundation, but this did not go anywhere.

Le Corbusier also attempted to gather funds, with the expressed intention of setting up his own foundation in the house. This project made a lot of headway, since in 1966, one year after the architect's death, the prefecture of Seine-et-Oise carried out a "feasibility investigation prior to the declaration of public utility for the construction of a Le Corbusier foundation." Finally, agreement was reached among all the parties, with the lycée being constructed and the Villa preserved, thanks to, it must be emphasized, the unfailing support of André Malraux. The procedure for registering the building in the National Register began in 1964, in Le Corbusier's lifetime, which is highly unusual. And the foundation was created, but in the Maison La Roche, built by the architect in Paris in 1924.

After two very long renovation campaigns, carried out first by Jean Dubuisson beginning in 1963 and then, from 1985 to 1992, by Jean-Louis Véret (one of those responsible for the preservation of the Villa), the house now receives hundreds of thousands of visitors a year from around the world. And I can't help thinking of my grandmother, who wanted to build a house that would survive her.

Building "Les Heures claires" – the sunny days – that was my grandparents' project, the utopian, never specifically formulated specification that Le Corbusier took hold of to build his house. This limitation – but was it really? – was undoubtedly what he needed at that time. It was less than a year after the lashing he had taken with the refusal of the Palace of Nations in Geneva that he had so marvelously described: "Our palace is set on the ground among the high stand of trees, surrounded by grass where it will not disturb even a wild rosebush." Maybe it was in Poissy, on the banks of the Seine, rather than on the shores of Lake Geneva, that Le Corbusier built his palace? The palace of sunny days.

The sunny days were fleeting. They never last, but the Villa Savoye is still there, the testimony to that utopia that an architect of genius captured in a white box delicately set on the ground, without disturbing even a wild rosebush.

BIBLIOGRAPHY

Les Heures claires
Proyecto y arquitectura en la Villa Saboye
de Le Corbusier y Pierre Jeanneret
Josep Quetglas

Associació d'idees. Centre d'investigations esthétiques, 2007
ISBN 84-87478-48-4

Le Corbusier, le grand
Jean-Louis Cohen, Tim Benton

Phaidon, 2008
ISBN 978-0-714-84668-2

The Villas of Le Corbusier and Pierre Jeanneret, 1920–1930
Tim Benton

Éditions de La Villette, 2007
ISBN 978-2-915456-06-7

Le Corbusier
Habiter : de la Villa Savoye à l'Unité d'habitation de Marseille
Jacques Sbriglio

Actes Sud, 2009
ISBN 978-2-7427-8392-2

Le Corbusier
Moments in the Life of a Great Architect
Arthur Ruegg, René Burri

Birkhäuser, 1999
ISBN 978-3-7643-5999-7

Le Corbusier – Complete Works in eight volumes
Willy Boesiger, Oscar Stonorov, Max Bill (Eds.)

Birkhäuser, 1995
ISBN 978-3-7643-5515-9

Le Corbusier. The Villa Savoye
Jacques Sbriglio

Birkhäuser, 2008
ISBN 978-3-7643-8230-8

IMPRINT

Texts: Jean-Marc Savoye
Illustrations: Jean-Philippe Delhomme
Layout, cover design: Roch Deniau
Translation from French into English:
Sheila Malovany-Chevallier
Copy editing: John Sweet
Project management: Baharak Tajbakhsh,
Alexander Felix
Production and typesetting: Heike Strempel
Paper: 150 g/m² Condat Matt Perigord
Printing: optimal media GmbH

Library of Congress Control Number: 2020930699

Bibliographic information published by the German
National Library
The German National Library lists this publication
in the Deutsche Nationalbibliografie; detailed
bibliographic data are available on the Internet at
http://dnb.dnb.de.

ISBN 978-3-0356-2061-0
e-ISBN (PDF) 978-3-0356-2063-4
German Print-ISBN 978-3-0356-2060-3

Original French Edition: «Les Heures claires de la
Villa Savoye», © 2015 Éditions les quatre chemins;
Illustrations: ©Jean Philippe Delhomme; License
conveyed by BOOKSAGENT – France (www.booksagent.fr)

© 2020 Birkhäuser Verlag GmbH, Basel
P.O. Box 44, 4009 Basel, Switzerland
Part of Walter de Gruyter GmbH, Berlin/Boston

9 8 7 6 5 4 3 2 1

www.birkhauser.com

Illustration credits

© J.-M. Savoye
↳ p. 4, 5, 12, 15, 28

Photograph, Martine Frank ©FLC-ADAGP
↳ p. 7

Letters, Fondation Le Corbusier ©FLC-ADAGP
↳ p. 10 – 11, 16, 38 – 40, 50 – 51

Plans and drawings, Fondation Le Corbusier
©FLC-ADAGP
↳ p. 14, 18 – 23

Photograph, Paul Kozlowski ©FLC-ADAGP
↳ p. 26

Photograph, Ernest Weissmann Archive ©FLC-ADAGP
↳ p. 32

Archives communales de Poissy (cote 48H3)
↳ p. 44, 49

Beauregard Catholic community newsletter
↳ p. 49

Photograph, Marius Gravot ©FLC-ADAGP
↳ p. 52